G
Nortl
Pu

Keith Wadd

COUNTRYSIDE BOOKS
NEWBURY BERKSHIRE

First published 2018
© Keith Wadd 2018

COUNTRYSIDE BOOKS
3 Catherine Road
Newbury, Berkshire

To view our complete range of books,
please visit us at
www.countrysidebooks.co.uk

ISBN 978 1 84674 357 3

Cover design by Barrie Appleby

Designed by KT Designs, St Helens
Produced through The Letterworks Ltd., Reading
Typeset by KT Designs, St Helens
Printed in Poland

Introduction

I have much appreciated the opportunity in this publication to re-visit all of the walks I described in the, now out of print, 2006 edition of *Pocket Pub Walks North Yorkshire*.

The book is an exploration of North Yorkshire on foot (and what better way of exploring!). It starts at Harrogate and explores the Yorkshire Dales, going as far west as Whernside (Yorkshire's highest peak), then looping round Swaledale in the north followed by some walks in the comparative lowlands of the county. Then from Brockadale in the far south, the tour visits the Yorkshire Wolds and the Howardian Hills and concludes with several walks in and around the North York Moors, including a trip to the seaside at Robin Hood's Bay. The final walk along Sutton Bank provides a grandstand finish.

The walks are a reminder of how beautiful the county is and of the rich variety of scenery and history within its boundaries. The book is also an accidental history lesson, particularly in industrial history and social change. It is easy to forget that a few generations ago North Yorkshire and the hills of northern England were a thriving and quite populous industrial area, mined and quarried for ironstone and alum, lead and even coal, as well as for building materials and roadstone, and criss-crossed by connecting railways. Virtually all of it has gone, and it is astonishing how

The Fountaine Inn, Linton-in-Craven

nature has so swiftly greened the old industrial sites. Several of the walks go past the sites of this former industrial activity.

At risk of telling experienced walkers what they already know, wear strong footwear (lightweight boots are ideal), make sure that you have waterproof clothing plus a hat (for the sun as well as the rain). It also makes good sense to carry an extra layer – several of the walks go up to 300m or more above sea level.

The welcoming pubs all sell good beer (much of it locally brewed), serve food, and many are residential (why not make a holiday of it?). If you wish to park in the pub car park, please ask in the pub beforehand. However, I have indicated another parking place nearby for all of the walks.

The walks should be free of path problems, but should you come across any please report them to the local authority at paths@northyorks. gov.uk.

Many thanks to Anne, my wife, for her good company on the walks, and for her much appreciated help and support in the preparation of this book.

Doing these walks has been a very enjoyable experience, and I hope they give the reader as much pleasure as they have given me. Happy walking!

Keith Wadd

Publisher's Note

We hope that you obtain considerable enjoyment from this book: great care has been taken in its preparation. However, changes of landlord and actual pub closures are sadly not uncommon. Likewise, although at the time of publication all routes followed public rights of way or permitted paths, diversion orders can be made and permissions withdrawn.

In order to assist in navigation to the start point of the walk, we have included the nearest postcode, although of course a postcode cannot always deliver you to a precise starting point, especially in rural areas.

We cannot, of course, be held responsible for such diversion orders or any inaccuracies in the text which result from these or any other changes to the routes, nor any damage which might result from walkers trespassing on private property. We are anxious, though, that all details covering the walks and the pubs are kept up to date, and would therefore welcome information from readers which would be relevant to future editions.

Valley Gardens and Pump Room

1 Harrogate

5 miles/8km

WALK HIGHLIGHTS

Harrogate sets the scene for this book because it is centrally placed and the walk provides wide views over the surrounding North Yorkshire countryside. Harrogate rose to prominence as a spa town in the 19th century, and it retains the fine buildings and spaciousness of its heyday. This well-wooded walk is close to the town but rarely near buildings.

THE PUB

The Old Bell, Royal Parade **HG1 2SZ**
☎ 01423 507930 www.markettowntaverns.co.uk

THE WALK

Go through the gateway of the **Valley Gardens** and along the path beside the stream. Go past **Bogs Field** (where 36 mineral springs, each one unique, come to the surface) and continue on a broad path up the hillside. Keep on the main path as you approach the **Pine Woods**, cross

Guide to North Yorkshire Pub Walks

HOW TO GET THERE AND PARKING: The Old Bell is on Royal Parade, more or less opposite the Pump Room Museum and close to the entrance to the Valley Gardens. There is no parking at the pub but there is pay and display parking nearby. For free parking, the best bet is to park on or near Kent Road (see map) beyond the meter/disc zone. The No.36 Leeds/Harrogate/Ripon bus service is every 10 minutes much of the day. **Sat Nav:** HG1 2SZ.

MAP: OS Explorer 289 Leeds or 297 Lower Wharfedale and Washburn Valley. **Grid Ref:** SE 297555.

a road, and go up the access road to **Harrogate Indoor Bowling Club**. Turn left after the greenhouses, past a stone water tower on the left and a charming square stone tower on the right (now used by the Astronomy Society). An extensive view unfolds leftwards across the Vale of York to the North York Moors and the Wolds.

2 Retrace your steps to the greenhouses and go straight on through a gap beside a metal gate. Soon slant left across a wide grassy area to join a broad path into the **Pine Woods**. After a short distance, wide views appear on the right (information board and telescope) including the Pennine hills enclosing Nidderdale backed by Buckden Pike (702m).

3 Turn right along the tarmac road at **Harlow Carr Gardens** (turn left for the entrance) then soon go left down a road marked "private" to the former **Harrogate Arms**. Go to the left of the former pub, turn right at the metal gate, cross a foul-smelling stream (another sulphurous Harrogate spring), and follow a wooded path. Shortly after a footbridge, turn right by a **Harrogate Ringway** sign (the Ringway is followed for the next two miles), descend steeply to cross a footbridge and boardwalk, then follow the woodland path as it climbs to a gap in the fence then bears right close to the fence/wall. Climb steps up to a footpath sign, and turn left along the top of rocks to **Birk Crag**, a splendid airy place.

4 Continue down a steep, stepped path, then bear right on a level track through attractive woodland to reach **Cornwall Road**. Turn left, ignore **Oakdale Mews**, then soon turn sharp right by the Ringway sign along a broad unsurfaced road. Turn left between houses 72 and 72A and follow

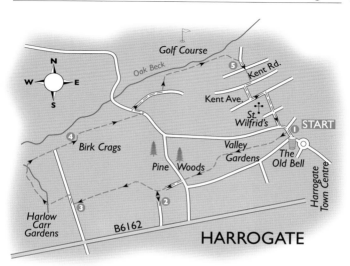

the path down to **Oak Beck** at the **Iron Bridge**, Harrogate's oldest bridge, not made of iron but reputedly used for carrying ironstone to nearby Kirkby Overblow. Keep the stream on the left as you follow the path down the wooded valley before it climbs up to a road.

Turn right up the hill (leaving the Ringway), then at the T-junction, go up the footpath straight ahead. Turn right along **Kent Road**, then first left down **Kent Avenue** with the large bulk of **St Wilfrid's church** (Grade I Listed) straight ahead. Turn left at the church, then turn right and along **Clarence Drive** to the **Valley Gardens**.

PLACES OF INTEREST NEARBY
Knaresborough, four miles away is a town of charm and interest. Most of its castle, on a spectacular cliff-top site overlooking the River Nidd, failed to survive the Civil War, but an impressive keep remains.

7

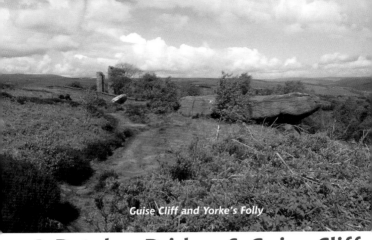
Guise Cliff and Yorke's Folly

2 Pateley Bridge & Guise Cliff

6 miles/9.6km

WALK HIGHLIGHTS
This is a walk in the Nidderdale, an Area of Outstanding Natural Beauty. Enjoy riverside walking by the River Nidd, a lake, a tarn and a pond, extensive woodland, an exhilarating gritstone edge, a folly, and many fine views. Nidderdale used to be a hive of industry with extensive lead-mining on the slopes of Greenhow Hill, widespread quarrying and a substantial linen industry.

THE PUB
The Royal Oak, Bridgehouse Gate, **HG3 5HG**
☎ 01423 711577

THE WALK
1 From **Nidd Walk Car Park** drop down to the path beside the **River Nidd**, turn left and follow it downstream for some attractive tree-lined riverside walking. After half a mile the path swings right and broadens into a lane with a large lake on the right.

HOW TO GET THERE AND PARKING: Take the B6165/B6265 from Ripley to Pateley Bridge. Follow B6265 down Pateley Bridge High Street and turn left immediately before the bridge for Nidd Walk Car Park (£1.40 all day). For the pub, cross the bridge and the Royal Oak is on the right after 200 metres. **Sat Nav:** HG3 5NA.

MAP: OS Explorer 298 Nidderdale. **Grid Ref:** SE 158655.

Turn right at the road (just below **Glasshouses** village) and go left at the road junction immediately after the bridge over the river. The large stone building across the river is the former **Glasshouses Mill**. After a few metres, fork right on a lane up the hillside. The lane becomes an enclosed footpath before entering **Parker Wood**. Go immediately right for a few metres and then continue up the hillside in attractive woodland on a clear path. Turn left at the T-junction of paths, then follow the main path as it swings right climbing quite steeply. **Guisecliff Tarn** is on the right. Shortly after the tarn, the path swings left, descends briefly, then takes a fairly level course through the wood. At the end of the wood the path climbs steeply up the hillside to a gate just to the left of a large mast (a good viewpoint with extensive views eastwards to Sutton Bank and the Yorkshire Wolds).

Turn right and along the fence round the back of the mast, go over a stile, then follow a well-trodden path on the top of **Guise Cliff**, a splendid airy walk along the gritstone edge with good views into Nidderdale. The notice "For Your Safety Keep To The Path" should not be taken lightly as there are fearsome crevices. The path eventually follows a wall on the right with views of **Greenhow Hill** ahead. After a gate in the wall, the path goes beside the bizarrely-shaped Yorke's Folly erected around 1800 to provide work at a time of local unemployment. Slant right on a rocky path to the nearby road.

Cross the road to a footpath gate and follow the path signposted to **Bewerley**. Soon the path enters **Skrikes Wood**, descending steeply. Ignore the stile at the bottom of the wood and go left beside the wall. The clear path, still in the wood, descends to a metal bridge over **Fosse Gill** to reach a road where you turn right.

Guide to North Yorkshire Pub Walks

5 After a few metres, turn left on a footpath which initially goes close to the road, then by an information board turns left into **Fishpond Wood**. The path goes by the fishpond and up to a footpath gate. Turn right and up some fine old steps to another footpath gate (good view). In the next field veer

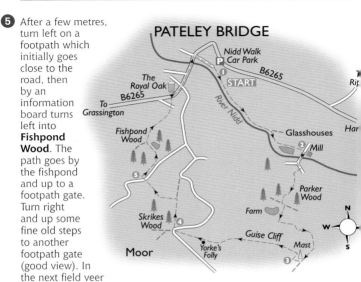

slightly right towards the bottom of the hill, cross the boardwalk to a footpath gate and then a road. Turn left along the road, then soon turn right (footpath sign) and slant across the field to the far corner to join the B6265. Turn right (no verge so beware traffic!) and continue down the B6265 into **Pateley Bridge** (the **Royal Oak** on the left). Immediately after the bridge over the river, turn right and follow the road to the car park. The impressive stone building on the left is a former railway station (Pateley Bridge had two!).

PLACES OF INTEREST NEARBY

The **Nidderdale Museum** at Pateley Bridge is an excellent small museum. Five miles away are **Brimham Rocks** (National Trust), a remarkable outcrop of gritstone rocks weathered into fantastic shapes.

Linton Falls

3 Linton Falls

5 miles/8km

WALK HIGHLIGHTS

A pretty Wharfedale walk in the Yorkshire Dales National Park. Linton village green with Linton Beck flowing through the middle is a delight, Linton Falls are spectacular, and there is enjoyable riverside walking by the River Wharfe.

THE PUB

The Fountaine Inn, Linton-in-Craven, **BD23 5HJ**
☎ 01756 752210 www.fountaineinnatlinton.co.uk

THE WALK

From the **Fountaine Inn**, take the path by the postbox and telephone box, cross the **Linton Beck** by the ancient packhorse bridge, turn left for a few metres, then right at a T-junction along a broad road. The road soon divides. Take the right turn, a narrow quiet lane. Turn right when it

HOW TO GET THERE AND PARKING: From Skipton follow the B6265 to Grassington. After six miles (just after large quarry on left) turn right for Linton which is reached in another mile. Park in the village close to Fountaine Inn. If no parking in the village, follow the road signposted to Linton Church and there is Pay and Display parking by point 2. **Sat Nav:** BD23 5HJ.

MAP: Outdoor Leisure 2 Yorkshire Dales Southern & Western areas. **Grid Ref:** SD 996626.

soon reaches a T-junction with the B6160, then almost immediately take the footpath on left "**Footpath to Linton Church and Falls ¼ mile**". The path follows the wall on the left and there are good views ahead. Turn left at a junction of paths, and left when a road is reached (right for **Linton Church**).

2 Follow the road past the toilets and car park and soon turn right on a path signed "**Linton Falls**". The walled path swings right immediately before a hump-back stone footbridge, and soon leads to a footpath over the Linton Falls, a stunning place particularly when the River Wharfe is high. The surrounding buildings were part of the former water-powered mill. Turn right immediately after the footbridge on a path signposted to **Hebden and Burnsall** (it is also the **Dales Way**, the long-distance path from Ilkley to Windermere). Turn right when a lane is reached, and continue along it till it peters out and becomes a footpath, then enjoy a mile of superb riverside walking by the **River Wharfe** as you follow the path down to **Hebden Suspension Bridge**.

3 Cross the bridge (an experience in itself), continue beside the river for a short distance and take the second footpath on the right which climbs a flight of steps and then becomes a delightful walled path. Turn right when a road (B6160) is reached, follow it for a short distance, then soon turn left on a walled lane (no sign, but just before a building on the left). Follow the lane for a short distance, then at a junction of footpaths (sign) struggle over a step stile and follow a clear path through meadows with good views of **Barden & Thorpe Fell** to the left. After crossing a stream, keep by the wall/fence on the right as the path goes to the far corner of the field. In the next field climb up to a gate then swing left along a

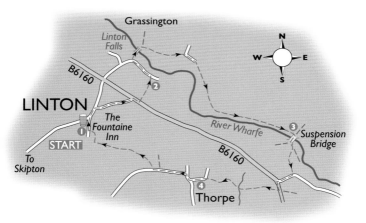

lane, soon to reach a metalled road where you turn left and drop into **Thorpe**.

Keep the village green on your left (but read the noticeboard about the maypole), then take the road on the right by the postbox. Soon turn left at a road junction and follow **Thorpe Lane**, a narrow metalled lane ("unsuitable for HGVs"), for half a mile and take the second path on the right (signposted "**Public footpath to Linton ¾ Mile**"). The path goes just to the right of a belt of trees, and then continues in the same direction with views of **Great Whernside** and **Buckden Pike** ahead. As the path descends to a farm take the third path on the right and go round the side of the farm buildings to reach a road. Turn right, and in a few steps you are back in **Linton**.

PLACES OF INTEREST NEARBY

What better than to stay in **Linton**! Just browse around the village green. There's an obelisk, 18th-century almshouses, and a delightful stream. **Linton's church** (near point 2) has Norman origins.

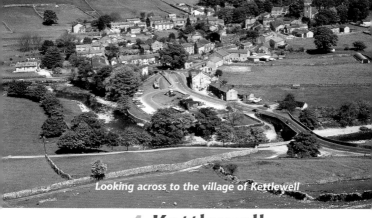

Looking across to the village of Kettlewell

4 Kettlewell

6 miles/9.6km

WALK HIGHLIGHTS

A walk in the magnificent limestone landscape of Upper Wharfedale: steep wooded hillsides full of flowers in spring, craggy limestone outcrops (called "scars"), and a mosaic of walled pastures. Rarely can the works of man have blended so well with nature (albeit accidentally). Be prepared for two long climbs. There are also several rocky bits where the use of hands is recommended.

THE PUB

The Racehorses Hotel, BD23 5QZ

☎ 01756 760233   www.racehorseshotel.co.uk

THE WALK

1 Leave **Kettlewell** by the Grassington road (B6160). Cross the bridge over the **River Wharfe**, and immediately beyond the left-hand bend take the path on the right "**Permissive Footpath Hawkswick 2¼ miles**". When the path forks (quarter of a mile) take the right-hand path which slants up the hillside through delightful woodland (spring flowers). After a footpath gate, keep to the wall on the right still climbing the hillside

HOW TO GET THERE AND PARKING: Take the B6265 from Skipton to Threshfield (near Grassington), then B6160 past spectacular Kilnsey Crag to Kettlewell. The Racehorses Hotel is on the B6160 immediately after the hump-back bridge. **Sat Nav:** BD23 5QZ

MAP: OS Explorer Outdoor Leisure 30 Yorkshire Dales: Northern & Central Areas. **Grid Ref:** SD 968722.

(**Gate Cote Scar**). After a gap in the wall slant left to a ladder stile (*NB: permissive path on OS map*). The path continues to climb, then levels out on upland pasture giving easy grassy walking. Where the path divides take either – reunion soon occurs. After a ladder stile, you can look down into **Wharfedale** and see **Kilnsey Crag**. The path swings right by a cairn and slants down the hillside into **Littondale** with fine views

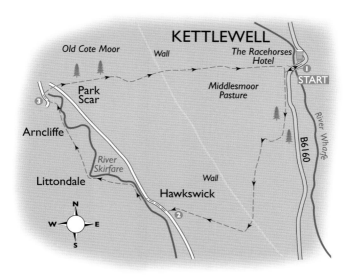

into the dale. The path comes into a walled lane, soon dropping into **Hawkswick**.

2 Turn right and along the road through Hawkswick. Shortly after the village, turn left across the footbridge over the **River Skirfare**, then immediately turn right along the riverbank on to the footpath to **Arncliffe**. The path crosses meadows before rejoining the river (in spring and summer you will see sand martins). Go to the right of a stone barn, through a gate to the left of a clump of trees, then veer right to rejoin the riverbank. The path enters Arncliffe between houses and to the left of the churchyard. The church has a 14th to 16th-century tower, the churchyard fine yews.

3 Turn right at the road, then take the footpath signposted to **Kettlewell** immediately after the bridge over the river. Cross another road, then let climbing commence! Take the clear path that slants up the hillside to a stone step stile, then continue in the same direction up the wooded slope of **Park Scar**, another good place for spring flowers. Glance back for outstanding views. The path becomes increasingly rocky but with care there is no serious difficulty. After a ladder stile, the path leaves the woodland and slants to the right as it continues to climb the hillside. Fairly soon there is a footpath gate, further on the path goes through a ruined wall. The heather moorland is perhaps a surprise after the limestone. As the path approaches the top of the **Old Cote Moor** ridge there are two gated step stiles. The path continues in the same direction as it makes the long descent to Kettlewell. There are stunning views: **Great Whernside** (704m) is straight ahead and the large hill to the left is **Buckden Pike** (702m). When a wall is reached, ignore the gate, and cross a ladder stile lower down. Further on, descent of **Gate Cote Scar** is via a rocky limestone cleft requiring the use of the hands in several places (avoid it by steering a few hundred metres to the left). Turn right at the junction of paths at the bottom of the hill (at last!) and the path soon leads to the bridge over the **Wharfe** and into **Kettlewell**.

PLACES OF INTEREST NEARBY

Kettlewell is an attractive village which formerly had a market and a cotton mill. **Grassington**, an engaging small town seven miles down the valley, houses the **Upper Wharfedale Museum** and the **Yorkshire Dales National Park Centre**.

The path along Giggleswick Scar

5 Giggleswick Scar

6 miles /9.6km

WALK HIGHLIGHTS

A limestone walk on paths of springy turf that are a delight to tread.
Giggleswick Scar, a limestone edge (with several caves), bordering the
great Craven Fault, is a particular feature. Each of the Three Peaks (Pen-
y-ghent, Ingleborough and Whernside) can be seen along the way, and
in the distance on a clear day, the Lake District hills.

THE PUB

The Harts Head Hotel, Giggleswick, **BD24 0BA**
☎ 01729 822086 www.hartsheadhotel.co.uk

THE WALK

After leaving the **Harts Head**, turn right down **Belle Hill** into
Giggleswick village. Turn right at the bottom and into the churchyard of
St Alkelda's (much of it 15th-century). Turn right after the churchyard
on to a lane, then left through a gap stile immediately after the last
house. Walk through the manicured grounds of **Giggleswick School** to
reach a tarmac road via a flight of steps. Turn right and follow the road
for about a third of a mile to the B6480.

Guide to North Yorkshire Pub Walks

HOW TO GET THERE AND PARKING: Giggleswick is 17 miles from Skipton. Follow the A65 Skipton-Kendall road, then turn right on B6840 through Settle to Giggleswick. The Harts Head is on the B6480 on the left. By train, Settle station (join the walk at point 5) is more convenient than Giggleswick station. Park on the B6480 by the Harts Head or on nearby streets. **Sat Nav:** BD24 0BA.

MAP: OS Explorer Outdoor Leisure 41 Forest of Bowland and Ribblesdale. **Grid Ref:** SD 813641.

2 Briefly turn right then after a few metres go left on a path signposted "**Buck How Brow 1½ miles**". The path soon climbs steeply beside the disused quarry on the left. Keep close to the boundary fence as the path goes round the top of the quarry. There are fine views of **Pen-y-ghent**. At the end of the quarry, take the left-hand path leading to a cairn (good viewpoint), then go right and enjoy for three quarters of a mile the undulating grassy path along **Giggleswick Scar**. There are fine views, and in summer a carpet of flowers, particularly the bright yellow rock rose. At the end of the scar, the path swings right to a footpath gate, then, after a brief steep climb up a field, **Ingleborough** rears up ahead, and beyond it, just to the right, a snatch of **Whernside**. In the distance to the left of Ingleborough the **Lakeland hills** can be seen. Continue through fields and after about half a mile soon after a farm gate, you come to a signpost.

3 Turn right on path signposted "**Stack House 1½ miles**". The path goes up the grassy hillside to a ladder stile by a gate, and in the next field to the left of the wall ahead and down to a farm gate. Continue in the same direction to another farm gate and (important!), a few metres after this, go through another gate on the right. Continue in the same direction (enjoyable grassy walking) with the wall now on the left. Keep in the same direction after the next gate and descend the rocky field to a gate in the bottom corner, immediately followed by another gate. Cross the next field to the left-hand ladder stile of the two available, then descend to a signpost.

4 Turn right and follow the track by the wall on the left. When **Stackhouse Lane** is reached on the left, keep in the field for a short distance, then (footpath gate) cross the lane to a path signposted "**Ribble Way Settle Bridge ¾ mile**". Continue along **Ribble Way** with the **River Ribble** often nearby. The path goes round the left side of a sports field to reach **Settle Bridge**. Cross the B6480 and follow the riverside path (interesting information boards) to a footbridge leading to **Settle** town centre.

Take the right-hand path that climbs the bank and leads into **Giggleswick**. Turn right when the road is reached, then right again up **Belle Hill** to the **Harts Head**.

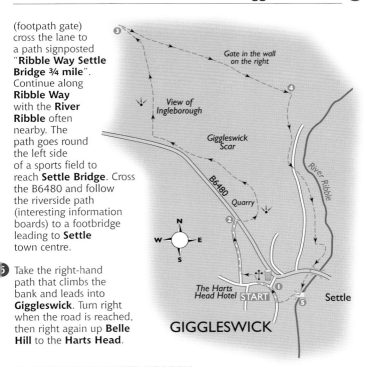

PLACES OF INTEREST NEARBY

Nearby **Settle** is a place of character whose market gained its charter in 1249. Settle is also the starting point of the famous **Settle-Carlisle railway**, a scenic route across the top of the Pennines.

Ribblehead Viaduct

6 Whernside & Ribblehead

8 miles/12.8km

WALK HIGHLIGHTS

This walk is an ascent of Whernside (736m), the highest peak in Yorkshire and one of the "Three Peaks". It's a grand Pennine walk with terrific views and a close-up of the famous Ribblehead Viaduct. The ascent is easy on a broad, firm path with scarcely a steep gradient. The descent is very steep and needs care. Take extra layers of clothing as it is usually a different climate on top.

THE PUB

The Station Inn, Ribblehead, **LA6 3AS**
☎ 01524 241274 www.stationinnribblehead.co.uk

THE WALK

1 From just below the **Station Inn** turn left along the bridleway signposted **Gunnerfleet Farm**, or from the T-junction take the path to the viaduct. The two routes soon join in a broad track to **Ribblehead Viaduct**. The whaleback shape of Whernside can be seen beyond the viaduct. Ribblehead Viaduct with its 24 arches of local limestone, built from 1870 to 1875, is the most impressive architectural feature on the Settle-

HOW TO GET THERE AND PARKING: From Settle take the B6479 up
  Ribblesdale to the T-junction with the B6255 at Ribblehead. Turn left
  for parking at the Station Inn which is already in view or park roadside
  at the T-junction. **Sat Nav:** LA6 3AS.

MAP: OS Explorer OL2 Yorkshire Dales Southern & Western areas. **Grid
  Ref:** SD 763791.

Carlisle line. Nearby, is the site of the camp where the workers who
built the viaduct lived. It housed over 2,000 people and had a school
and library. The work was hard and dangerous and many died; their
unmarked graves are in the churchyard at nearby **Chapel le Dale**.

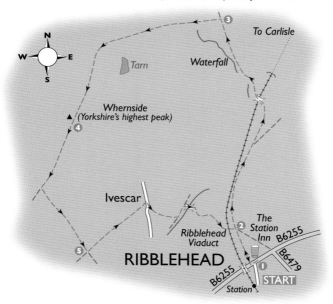

2 Follow the track to the right of the viaduct and up the hillside beyond. Bear left when the track divides and cross **Little Dale Beck** by a footbridge. Cross the bridge over the railway and keep to the main broad path as it climbs steadily to the right of **Force Gill** and its fine waterfall.

3 Go over the stile on the left (signposted **Whernside 1¾ miles**) and continue climbing. There is an unnamed tarn on the left and peat hags all around. The path swings left and eventually reaches the Whernside ridge. Nip up to the wall on the right for the best views into **Dentdale**.

4 Whernside's summit is not a peak but a trig point over the wall by the shelter. The all-round view is outstanding. The table-top of Ingleborough dominates the scene straight ahead to the south, with **Pendle Hill** beyond. To the right is **Morecambe Bay**. Further round are the Howgills and the Lake District fells. To the east are Pen Hill, Buckden Pike and Great Whernside ("great" but not as high!). After admiring the view, continue going along the ridge which falls in a series of gigantic steps. After the last one, follow the main path which drops very steeply. It is now advisable to ignore the view, and watch where you're putting your feet.

5 At the bottom of the descent at a crossroads of paths by a stone barn, turn left on the path signposted to **Winterscales**. The path (level walking!) goes just to the right of former farm buildings and continues in the same direction through fields just below a limestone scar. Turn sharp right in the farmyard at **Ivescar**, then immediately after a barn go over a step stile on the left (signposted "**public footpath**"). Walk diagonally across the field to a step stile and continue up a small hill and down the other side keeping the wall on your left. Go over the stile in the left corner of the next field, then cross the following field to a ladder stile just beyond the right-hand pylon. Go left along the road for a few metres, then turn right (signposted to **Ribblehead**) over the bridge across **Little Dale Beck**. Now follow the farm access road which goes under the massive arches of **Ribblehead Viaduct** and back to the **Station Inn**.

PLACES OF INTEREST NEARBY

Opposite the Station Inn is the **Ribblehead Visitor Centre**. On the B6255 road to Ingleton are the White Scar caves. **Ingleton** is at the junction of the rivers Doe and Twiss and both have impressive waterfalls within easy walking distance.

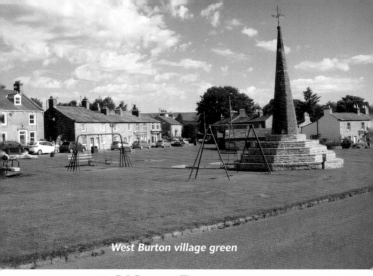
West Burton village green

7 West Burton

3 miles or 4 miles/4.8km or 6.4km

WALK HIGHLIGHTS

A waterfall (watch out for a dipper or grey wagtail), woodland, meadows, an enjoyable green lane, glorious Wensleydale views, plus the pretty village of West Burton. The route slants up Morpeth Scar and the climb is rarely steep, but hang on for the rapid descent from the top of Hudson Quarry Lane.

THE PUB

The Fox & Hounds, West Burton, **DL8 4JY**
☎ 01969 663111 www.foxandhoundswestburton.co.uk

THE WALK

From the pub, go down to the bottom right-hand corner of the green, and turn down a lane signposted "**Waterfall**" to an attractive open area by the **Walden Beck** (information board) and an impressive waterfall

HOW TO GET THERE AND PARKING: Take the A684 along Wensleydale, and six miles west of Leyburn turn left to West Burton on the B6160. After almost two miles turn left into West Burton village. West Burton may also be reached from Wharfedale via the B6160. The Fox & Hounds pub is on the village green. There is road parking by the village green. **Sat Nav:** DL8 4JY.

MAP: OS EXPLORER Outdoor Leisure 30 Yorkshire Dales Northern & Central areas. **Grid Ref:** SE 017867.

100m upstream. Cross the stream by the footbridge and bear left climbing steeply. Follow the path up the field by the right of a stone barn to a footpath gate into a wood.

2 Turn left, signposted "**Morpeth Lane**", on an attractive woodland path by a fence on the left. Turn right when Morpeth Lane (aka Morpeth Gate) is reached and follow it up the hillside. Although stony, the lane is tree-lined and pleasant with increasingly good views. At one point **Bolton Castle** can be seen. After about half a mile, the rock face of **Morpeth Scar** is on the right.

3 At the top of the scar, turn right at the footpath sign pointing to "**West Burton via Hudson Quarry Lane**". The view is particularly fine here, **Wensleydale** to the right, **Bishopdale** to the left, and **Addlebrough** the table-top hill ahead. Continue along **Hudson Quarry Lane** which soon becomes an enjoyable green lane with fine views. The lane leaves its walls and goes across the top of two fields to reach a signpost by a wall end. Straight ahead is the **Walden Beck valley** with **Buckden Pike** (702m) at the far end.

4 Turn right and follow the steep path down the hillside. Make for a post and then a gate stile. The views continue to be a delight with **West Burton** almost at your feet in the valley below. The path zigzags down **Morpeth Scar** to a gap in a wall, then briefly veers right to a stile into woodland. The woodland path continues to descend steeply to reach the **Morpeth Lane** signpost (easily missed – watch carefully!) at point 2.

5 Retrace your steps on the path down the field soon to reach a signpost at the corner of a wall. For the shorter walk (3 miles) carry straight on and retrace steps into **West Burton**. For the longer walk (4 miles), turn left on the path signposted "**Rookwith Bridge Cote Bridge**", a pleasant, clear and fairly level path across several meadows. It passes to the left of a house (**Riddings**), and in the following field

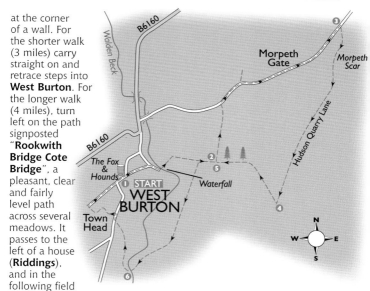

(barn on right) veer slightly right. In the next field keep to the wall on the right for a few metres to a footpath gate, then over a further field to cross the **Walden Beck** by a substantial footbridge.

Slant right (footpath sign "**West Burton**") up the hillside to reach a road at the far corner of the field. Turn right briefly, then turn left along a lane signposted "**Town Head 200 Yds**". Turn right when the farm at **Town Head** is reached, and walk down the road into **West Burton**.

PLACES OF INTEREST NEARBY

Two miles away the River Ure tumbles over the spectacular **Aysgarth Falls**, which comprise the Top Force, Middle Force, and Lower Force. There are well signposted paths for appreciative viewing. Nearby **Aysgarth church** claims to have the largest churchyard in the country.

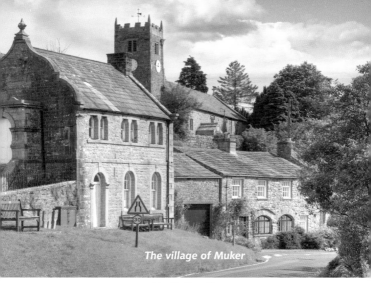

The village of Muker

8 Muker

6 miles/9.6km

WALK HIGHLIGHTS

A beautiful walk in spectacular Swaledale countryside. There are glorious Pennine views, limestone cliffs, waterfalls, and two attractive and interesting villages. Part of the route is on a section of the Pennine Way – a fine terrace path high above the valley.

THE PUB

The Farmers Arms, Muker **DL11 6QG**
☎ 01748 886297 www.farmersarmsmuker.co.uk

THE WALK

1 Turn left after leaving the car park, cross the fine bridge over the **Straw Beck**, and follow the road into **Muker** village. At the small green open

HOW TO GET THERE AND PARKING: Muker is at the far (western) end of Swaledale, eight miles from Reeth along the B6270. There is a car park on the left (£4.50 all day) at the entrance to Muker village. There are toilets (20p) in the village. **Sat Nav:** DL11 6QG.

MAP: OS Explorer Outdoor Leisure 30 Yorkshire Dales Northern & Central areas. **Grid Ref:** SD 909978.

space, turn right and walk up the road past the charming small building that was the former Literary Institute. Go to the right of a house called "**Armsleigh**" and just round the corner there is an excellent information board about the stone field barns that grace the local hillsides. Keep to the left of the postbox then follow a lane signposted "**Public Footpath to Keld**". The lane soon becomes a track, turns sharply left and zigzags up the hillside climbing steeply. Keep straight on when the track turns left through a gate, and soon the path joins the **Pennine Way** (footpath sign).

❷ Turn right and follow the Pennine Way along

27

a terrace route on the side of **Kisdon Hill**. There are stunning views into the valley below. The path is a glorious stretch of walking, but needs some care as it is rocky underfoot. Keep to the Pennine Way at all path junctions, (though if you have time and energy you may wish to turn off to visit the Kisdon Falls). Nearly two miles after point 2 you come to a junction of paths (signpost) where the Pennine Way turns right.

③ Turn right and continue along the Pennine Way (now also the **Coast to Coast Walk**) as it descends the hillside and crosses the **River Swale** (an idyllic spot) then go up the hillside for a short distance to view **East Gill Force waterfall** (another idyllic spot – and seats provided). Eventually drag yourself away from the stunning scene, retrace steps to the junction of paths at point 3 and turn right, soon to reach **Keld**. Don't miss the information board – in the heyday of lead mining, Keld was a much larger place. Turn left along the village street, left at the road junction by the public conveniences (another 20p), and left along the B6270 for a short distance.

④ Turn left along a track signposted "**Public Bridleway Muker 2½ miles**". After a brief descent, the track climbs up the side of Kisdon Hill and it is quite a steep climb. Ignore side paths. When the crushed-stone track turns left to a house, keep straight on along a wide grassy path and through the farm gate ahead. Now follow the grassy path for about a mile as it crosses **Kisdon Hill** (at about 480m) – enjoyable easy walking with good views including **Great Shunner Fell** to the far right. The path then drops steeply with fine views into **Swaledale**. Go left when you meet the Pennine Way again (signpost) and after a few metres return to point 2 from where you go down the hill back to **Muker**.

PLACES OF INTEREST NEARBY

The folk museum at **Reeth** contains many items of interest from Swaledale's former lead mining industry.

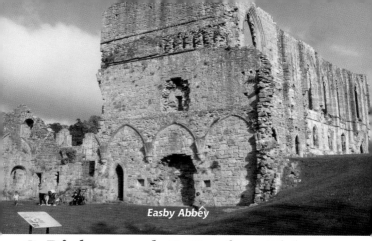

Easby Abbey

9 Richmond & Easby Abbey

3 miles/4.8km

WALK HIGHLIGHTS

This short walk is a mere tiddler, but it's a really nice one. Explore well-wooded paths within sight and sound of the River Swale, Easby Abbey, an ancient church, and spectacular views of Richmond Castle.

THE PUB

The Castle Tavern, Market Place, Richmond, **DL10 4HU**
☎ 01748 826931   www.castletavernrichmond.com

THE WALK

The start is a 10-minute walk from the car park. Exit the car park on to **Hurgill Road**, turn left on to **Victoria Road**, past the cricket pitch on your left. Turn right past the **Georgian Theatre Royal** and **Market Place** is at the bottom of that road.

Start from **Market Place**, and leave by the road in the top left corner that goes between the **Bishop Blaize** pub and the **Talbot Hotel**. Don't

Guide to North Yorkshire Pub Walks

HOW TO GET THERE AND PARKING: Leave the A1(M) at either Junction 52 (A6136 to Richmond) or Junction 53 (A6108 to Richmond). Park in Nuns Close Long Stay Car Park, Hurgill Road off Victoria Road (A6108 to Leyburn). All day £4.50. **Sat Nav:** DL10 4UN.

MAP: OS Explorer 304 Darlington & Richmond. **Grid Ref:** NZ 172009.

go down the hill on New Road but go straight on along a path signed "**To Castle Walls**" and past **Wardhorne Lettings and Gallery**. On the right there are good views up the valley. When the path swings left by the castle walls (which you may wish to visit en route), turn right down steep steps and continue down the steps to the road beside the **River Swale** at the bottom. Turn right, soon to reach the splendid bridge across the Swale.

2 Turn left across the bridge, but linger awhile to enjoy the fine view of the river and castle. Almost immediately after the bridge, turn left on the path signed "**Coast to Coast**" and go to the left of **Richmond Town Football Club** – such a pretty pitch that players could be excused for taking their eye off the ball. Continue along the riverside path (called "**Woodland Walk**"). At the end of the first field, ignore the path on the right and go through the footpath gate beside the farm gate. Follow the path down to an impressive road bridge (**Mercury Bridge**) which you go under, then turn right up the steps to the former station (a splendid conversion with shops, café, cinema, toilets, and lively scene).

3 Go to the left of the station, keep straight on and soon you are on the wide, tree-lined track that was formerly the railway to Darlington. Follow the former railway line until immediately after it crosses the **River Swale** (about a mile) then turn sharp left on a woodland lane that soon leads to the car park at **Easby Church**. Pop inside the ancient church which, though substantially Norman, has Anglo-Saxon origins. There are some fine medieval wall paintings.

4 Turn left and almost immediately the substantial limestone ruins of Easby Abbey rear up on the right. It dates from the late 12th century. It is maintained by English Heritage and entry is free. Continue along the path which soon leads into a field. Keep to the left-hand side, and soon go through a footpath gate on to the wooded banks of the Swale. The

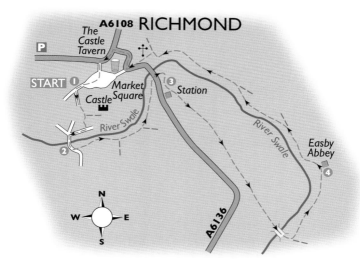

path bifurcates here and you can choose either. The left-hand riverside route is probably preferable unless the river is in spate. The paths reunite by the **Drummer Boy** stone and then you follow a lane high above the Swale with, at one point, a good view of **Richmond Castle**. When houses are reached, follow the lane that climbs to the right of the churchyard, then turn left through the churchyard to the road (**Station Road**). Turn right, then when the road swings right, turn left along **Frenchgate** and into **Richmond Market Place**.

PLACES OF INTEREST NEARBY

Browse round **Richmond** – of particular interest are the Norman castle on an impressive site overlooking the River Swale, and the Georgian Theatre Royal. A few miles to the north near Stanwick are the impressive earthworks of what was the capital of the Brigantes, the most powerful group in pre-Roman Britain.

The Black Bull in Boroughbridge

10 Boroughbridge & Aldborough

4 miles/6.4km

WALK HIGHLIGHTS

Boroughbridge and Aldborough are rich in interest, and the walk explores them both. Dere Street, the Roman road to Hadrian's Wall crossed the River Ure at Boroughbridge, and so did the Great North Road. On the outskirts of the town are the mysterious Devil's Arrows. Nearby Aldborough is a former Roman town.

THE PUB

The Black Bull Inn, St James Square, **YO51 9AR**
☎ 01423 322413 www.blackbullboroughbridge.co.uk

THE WALK

1 From the car park, carry straight on past the war memorial in **Hall Square** (note the butter market at the back) and along **Fishergate**. At the T-Junction turn right along **Bridge Street**. This was the Great

32

HOW TO GET THERE AND PARKING: Leave the A1(M) at Junction 48 and in half a mile you are on the main street in the middle of Boroughbridge. Turn right along Fishergate, then left into Hall Square for car parking (honesty box). Fishergate turns into High Street and you'll find the Black Bull at the top of this road. **Sat Nav:** YO51 9AR.

MAP: OS Explorer 299 Ripon & Boroughbridge. **Grid Ref:** SE 397667.

North Road and, in coaching times, the Crown Hotel on the right had stabling for 100 horses. Go across the bridge over the **River Ure**, built in 1562 and widened in 1784, and then cross **Milby Cut**, built around 1770 to enable boats to by-pass the Boroughbridge rapids. Beyond the roundabout was the former Boroughbridge railway station; the last train ran in 1964. Retrace your steps across the bridge, and note the plaque commemorating the Battle of Boroughbridge 1322.

A few metres after the **Three Horse Shoes**, turn right along **Valuation Lane** (easily missed). Continue along the lane to the end. There is a gap for walkers to the right of the forbidding metal gate. Turn left along the road. Two of the Devil's Arrows are across the field on the right. The road

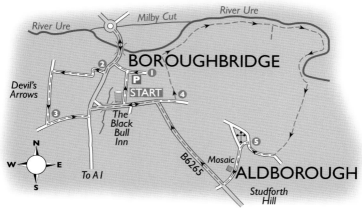

comes out at a T-junction with a third Devil's Arrow at the far side. The enormous stone monoliths were transported from the Knaresborough area (one wonders how!) around 2700BC.

3 Turn left at the T-junction. The road soon comes on to **Horsefair**, a reminder of Barnaby Fair where 14 days of horse trading used to take place every June. Cross Horsefair and continue straight ahead to the **Black Bull** pub (en route you cross Boroughbridge's other river, the Tutt, by a bridge said to contain a fourth Devil's Arrow). Keep straight on along **St James Square**, past the splendid octagonal-roofed well on the left, then soon turn left along **Aldborough Road**.

4 After 100m, turn left (footpath sign) along an enclosed path. The path goes under the canopy of a magnificent copper beech then continues along the floodbank of the **Ure**, nice open walking with big skies, reminiscent of the Fens. After a mile, the path comes out on to a tree-lined lane, which you follow until it reaches a road (formerly the Roman road from York). Turn right and walk into **Aldborough**.

5 Keep straight on at the road junction, then go through the gate on the left into the churchyard. The 14th-century church (I recommend a look inside) is in the middle of the former Roman town, possibly on the site of a temple of Mercury. Leave the churchyard by the path facing the church porch, turn left, and continue up the road by the attractive village green. At the top of the green are stocks and "The Old Courthouse of the Ancient Borough of Aldborough and Boroughbridge at which the members of Parliament were elected till 1832" (see plaque). The famous 1832 Reform Act abolished parliamentary seats such as this and redistributed them to unrepresented industrial towns. There is also a touching plaque to seven airmen (the oldest was 24!) killed in a tragic nearby aircrash in 1944. Continue up the road. On the right is the Roman mosaic (English Heritage, open 1 April to 30 September). **Studforth Hill**, on the left is thought to be the site of a Roman amphitheatre. Turn right at the crossroads and walk down the road (Pennine views) back to **Boroughbridge**.

PLACES OF INTEREST NEARBY
Ripon (6 miles) has a fine cathedral and interesting museums.

Long Crag and Brockadale

11 Kirk Smeaton & Brockadale

4 miles/6.4km

WALK HIGHLIGHTS

You can't get much further south in North Yorkshire than here! Those inside the thousands of vehicles on the A1 that whizz across Wentbridge Viaduct every day catch but a glimpse of beautiful Brockadale below. It is a deep wooded valley, almost a gorge in places, where the River Went cuts through the narrow band of magnesian limestone that runs right through lowland Yorkshire. Much of it is now protected by the Yorkshire Wildlife Trust. The best time to do this walk is in April with bluebells in the woods, and cowslips and orchids in the meadows.

The four-mile walk is a figure of eight, so for an enjoyable two-mile shorter walk just do the first circle and return to Kirk Smeaton from point 3.

THE PUB

The Shoulder of Mutton, Kirk Smeaton, **WF8 3JY**
☎ 01977 620348 (advisable to order sandwiches in advance)

Guide to North Yorkshire Pub Walks

HOW TO GET THERE AND PARKING: Kirk Smeaton is two miles east of the A1 between Ferrybridge and Doncaster. Leave the A1 immediately to the south of Wentbridge Viaduct. On entering Kirk Smeaton, turn left for the Shoulder of Mutton, which is in the middle of the village near to the church and small car park. **Sat Nav:** WF8 3JY.

MAP: OS Explorer 279 Doncaster, with a smidgeon of 278 Sheffield & Barnsley. **Grid Ref:** SE 519166.

THE WALK

1 From the car park take the path to the nearby church, a pleasant building in local stone with a squat tower. Follow the path round the left of the church to a fine old stone step stile. Turn left down the lane at the other side, which soon becomes an attractive path as it crosses the **River Went** and climbs into **Little Smeaton**.

2 Turn sharp left along **Chapel Lane**, then after a few metres go along on the enclosed path that initially runs parallel with the lane. Beware dog mess and avoid all side turns. There is a good view of **Brockadale** from **Long Crag**, a limestone crag just to the left of the path. At the Yorkshire Wildlife Trust information board the path gradually descends a meadow to reach the valley bottom. Cross the bridge over the River Went and go along the boardwalk to a crossroads of paths by an information board.

3 Turn right and follow the valley upstream into **Brockadale** The path soon enters woodland (**Sayle's Plantation**). In April and early May it is full of bluebells and wood anemones. Follow the wooded path through Brockadale for over a mile, a delightful stretch of riverside walking. Ignore paths that slant up the hillside.

4 About 100m before you go under the viaduct, turn left at a waymark post (easily missed) on a path that goes straight up the wooded hillside. Just before you reach the top, and still in woodland, turn sharp left (decrepit waymark post) along a faint woodland path in a slight hollow. When the path enters a field, continue in the same direction to the far corner and turn left along **Went Edge Road** (if the path is obstructed by crops or ploughing, go round the field to the right). Continue along Went Edge Road (quite busy) for just over half a mile with wide views ahead

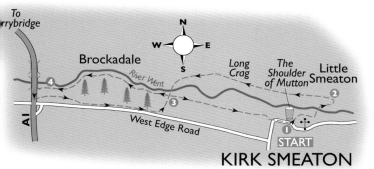

of lowland Yorkshire. Shortly after the pylons, go through a footpath gate on the left (footpath sign) and follow the path through a flower meadow (orchids in spring) to the junction of paths at point 3. Turn right here along a path that wends its way through woodland, meadow and scrub before climbing up a short hill to a road. Turn left and the **Shoulder of Mutton** is a mere few metres away.

PLACES OF INTEREST NEARBY

7 miles away at **Pontefract** is the famous castle (though not much of it remains) where Richard II died.

Thixendale

12 Thixendale
4 miles or 8 miles/6.4km or 12.8km

WALK HIGHLIGHTS
This walk from Thixendale explores some of the best of the Yorkshire Wolds countryside, a chalky downland landscape of steep-sided narrow valleys and airy uplands with wide views. The four-mile route is attractive and varied. It can be easily extended to eight miles to include Wharram Percy (which can also be visited by car).

THE PUB
The Cross Keys, Thixendale, **YO17 9TG**
☎ 01377 288272

THE WALK
1 Continue along the cul-de-sac road past the **Cross Keys**. Go through the footpath gate signposted "**Centenary Way**" and after the cricket pavilion follow the path on the left side of the valley. Go over a stile and continue in the same direction to a footpath gate just to the left of white gates. The path turns left gently climbing the side of **Court Dale**, full of flowers and butterflies in summer. After a footpath gate keep by the hedge on the left, and then turn left (signpost) along a track. After a quarter of a mile look out for sign on right where bridleway leaves the main track.

HOW TO GET THERE AND PARKING: Thixendale is 18 miles north east of York. Follow the A166 York-Bridlington road and turn left at Fridaythorpe. Park in Thixendale village near the Cross Keys. **Sat Nav:** YO17 9TG.

MAP: OS Explorer 300 Howardian Hills and Malton. **Grid Ref:** SE 845610.

For the four-mile walk keep straight on along the main track (Centenary Way). After it swings right, the path goes to the right of the hedge to a T-junction of paths at point 5 where the **Wolds Way** is joined.

For the eight-mile route, leave the Centenary Way at point 2 and follow the bridleway on the right, first through a belt of trees, then along

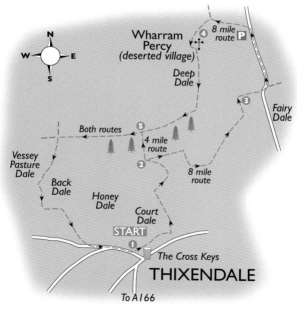

a field by a hedge on the left. Turn right in the next field then swing left (footpath sign) along the side of the field by a plantation on the right. Go through a gap in the hedge and turn left on a broad track with views of **Fairy Dale**. Ignore the track when it swings right and turn left (sign) keeping the hedge on the left through two fields to reach a T-junction of paths.

3 Turn right along a track soon to reach a tarmac road where you turn left. It's a quiet lane with good views northwards to Malton and the North York Moors. After approximately half a mile, turn left at a car park and follow the **Wolds Way** path down to the deserted medieval village of **Wharram Percy**.

4 The path goes to the right of the ruined church and the left of the pond, before climbing the side of the **Deep Dale** valley. Keep by the fence on the left with views of Deep Dale below. Turn right at the junction of paths, and still on the **Wolds Way**, follow a broad, grassy track which keeps close to the hedge/fence on the left to reach the junction of paths at point 5 at the beginning of a belt of trees.

5 Continue in the same direction (turn left if on four-mile walk) for half a mile to a junction of paths where a farm access track comes in from the right. Turn left on a path (**Wolds Way and Centenary Way**) that goes through some trees then follows a hedge on the left before dropping steeply into the **Vessey Pasture Dale**, enjoyable walking in a typical Wolds valley. The path goes through a footpath gate at the bottom, swings left to another gate, then climbs steeply out of the dale by a fence/hedge on the right. The path keeps the hedge on the right as it rounds an arable field at the top of the hill then crosses the hedge (stile now missing) and follows a track to the right of a small wood (ignore the track into the wood). The track then drops down into **Thixendale** with fine views of the valley. Turn left when the road is reached and walk through the village to the **Cross Keys**.

PLACES OF INTEREST NEARBY

Wharram Percy is a deserted medieval village dating from the 10th to the 12th century on a site that has been used since pre-Roman times. It is maintained by English Heritage.

Nunnington Hall

13 Nunnington & Caulkleys Bank

4.5 miles or 5.5 miles/7.2km or 8.8km

WALK HIGHLIGHTS

This walk explores as rural a stretch of countryside as can be found anywhere in England. Whichever direction takes the eye, there is an endless vista of fields, woods and low hills, and there is scarcely a blot on the landscape. Caulkleys Bank is a wooded chalky ridge, which provides enjoyable walking and extensive views. The walk takes you beside the River Rye and on pleasant green lanes. The longer route uses a path in the delightful Caulkleys Wood.

THE PUB

The Malt Shovel, Main Street, Hovingham, **YO62 4LF**
☎ 01653 628264 www.themaltshovelhovingham.uk

THE WALK

Go through the gate into the churchyard and round the 13th-century church to a footpath gate at the far end of the churchyard. Slant left down the field to a lane. Go straight across to a path beside a wall, then diagonally left across two fields to a road.

Guide to North Yorkshire Pub Walks

HOW TO GET THERE AND PARKING: Take the B1257 Malton Hemsley road, and one mile on the Helmsley side of Hovingham turn right to Nunnington which is a mile away at the other side of Caulkleys Bank. Park in Nunnington village near the church. **Sat Nav:** YO62 5US. The Malt Shovel is a five-minute drive away to the south.

MAP: OS Explorer 300 Howardian Hills and Malton. **Grid Ref:** SE 665790.

2 Turn right for a few metres then left along a footpath. Keep fairly close to the bottom of the field (a fine lime tree is passed), and cross into the next field just to the right of imposing stone gateposts. Make for the left-hand corner of the second field, a pleasant spot by the **River Rye**, then in the next field make for the gap between the two buildings

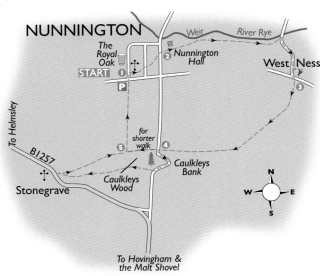

ahead at **Mill Farm** (the left-hand building is the former mill). Keep in the same direction through the farmyard and continue along a path past fine beeches at the bottom of a field. The path is through fields close to the River Rye on the left and comes out at **Ness Bridge** by the bridge over the river. Turn right on the road through **West Ness** to a T-junction (after a short distance you may avoid the road by turning left on the path signposted to **East Ness** then almost immediately take the permissive path on the right that continues through The Woodland Trust's **Joan's Wood** to the T-junction).

3 At the T-junction go straight across left and follow an enclosed track which soon becomes an attractive green lane (**Caulkleys Lane**) with increasingly wide views. Turn left briefly when it reaches a farm track (two-thirds of a mile) then almost immediately turn right at a bridleway sign. The path runs along the top of **Caulkleys Bank** passing a trig point on the right before reaching a road.

4 For the shorter version of the walk, cross the road and continue along the attractive path on the top of Caulkleys Bank (extensive views) to the footpath signpost at point 5.

    For the longer walk, turn left down the road (quite busy) for a quarter of a mile and, at the bottom of the hill, turn right on a bridleway signposted to **Stonegrave**. Follow the path through the delightful mixed woodland of **Caulkleys Wood**, and then continue in the same direction by a fence at the bottom of a field. Just before a stile beside a metal farm gate, turn sharp right and gradually ascend the hillside on a grassy track. Go through a gate and follow the track to the left of the wood, eventually to reach the signpost at point 5.

5 Turn left (if on the shorter route, turn right) and follow the broad track down into **Nunnington**. The track enters the village by the church.

PLACES OF INTEREST NEARBY

Nunnington Hall (National Trust) is a 17th-century manor house with a fine oak-panelled hall and many atmospheric rooms including a haunted one. The gardens are noted for their borders and orchards of traditional fruit varieties (**YO62 5UY**, ☎ 01439 748283).

Rosedale

14 Rosedale Abbey

5 miles/8km

WALK HIGHLIGHTS
Pleasant walking in the valley, moorland walking with good views, and some interesting industrial remains. Rosedale Abbey is a pretty village deep in the North York Moors. Little of the abbey remains, but you'll find a bit by the church.

THE PUB
The Coach House Inn, Rosedale Abbey, **YO18 8SD**
☎ 01751 417208 www.coachhouseinn.co.uk

THE WALK
1 From either of the two road junctions in the village follow the signs to "**Toilets**" and "**Castleton**". Turn left immediately after the toilets and soon take the footpath on the right signposted "**Dunn Carr Bridge**". Continue along the access road in the caravan park with the public footpath clearly signed. After a kissing gate, the path keeps close to the hedge on the left before descending into the valley bottom.

HOW TO GET THERE AND PARKING: Leave the A170 at Wrelton, two miles west of Pickering, and take the minor road to Cropton and Rosedale Abbey. The pub is on the right as you enter the village. There is street parking available. **Sat Nav:** YO18 8SD.

MAP: OS Explorer Outdoor Leisure 26 North York Moors Western area. **Grid Ref:** SE 725957.

At the junction of paths by the stream (**River Seven**), keep straight on by a fence on the left and into meadowland. Immediately after a gate, turn left on a track, and after a brief descent go through a footpath gate on the right. Keep close to the fence on the left then cross the stream by the footbridge (an attractive spot). Go up the hillside, through the gate between two farm buildings at **Low Thorgill Farm** (footpath sign), then straight on through the farmyard and along a lane.

Turn right when the tarmac road is reached and when it bends right keep straight on up a lane (public footpath sign). Just before the turning circle,

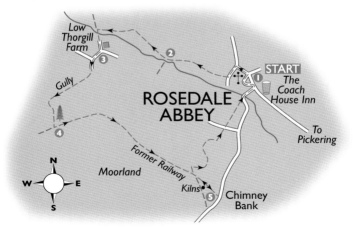

bear left on a narrow path that leads on to the moor (access land). Bear right and keep to the top of a gully on the right as you climb steadily. The path goes past a wall corner and, still climbing, soon bends left along a gully. Look for an isolated tree on the right and go immediately to the right of it, then follow a path up the hillside and keep straight on through heather soon to reach a broad track. The gullies are probably a relic of iron ore quarrying.

4 Turn left along the track, a former railway. It is enjoyable moorland walking (even more so when the heather is in full bloom) with attractive views of the valley below. After a while you reach a seat inscribed "In the dark, working hard, loading up the wooden cart Work shift over, in the sun, on the hill having fun". When you come to houses on the left, keep straight on along a crushed-stone footpath that soon leads to the impressive stone arches housing the kilns of the former Rosedale Iron Works.

Iron ore extraction in Rosedale took place between 1856 and 1929. The kilns roasted the ore to eliminate water and gas, and make it much more economic to transport. Initially the ore went by road to Pickering, then by rail to Whitby. The railway just walked along was constructed to link Rosedale Iron Works to the wider railway network via the Battersby Incline.

5 Retrace your steps to just past the houses, then go down the bank on the right to three ash trees. Continue down the hill to a fence where you turn left. The path keeps by the fence as it descends the hillside. Care is needed in places. The path goes round the corner of a golf course then over a stile on to the course. Follow the stakes, then turn left down to an access road. Cross the road at the bottom and descend the field by the hedge on the right. Go down steep steps into the garden of a house, then left along the road. In a few metres you are back in **Rosedale Abbey**.

PLACES OF INTEREST NEARBY

Some four miles away via Chimney Bank is **Ryedale Folk Museum** at Hutton-le-Hole. The church at nearby **Lastingham** has a celebrated Norman crypt.

Forge Valley, Sea Cut, and Raincliffe Woods

15 Forge Valley

5 miles/8km

WALK HIGHLIGHTS

Not many people who go to Scarborough know what's at the back of it all. The answer is the Forge Valley, Scarborough's hidden gem: a delightful valley with extensive mixed woodlands that are now a National Nature Reserve. Try the walk in early November when the autumn leaves are at their best. Forge Valley takes its name from 14th-century iron forges, which used charcoal from the local woodland.

THE PUB

Ye Olde Forge Valley Inn, West Ayton, **YO13 9JE**
☎ 01723 862146 www.yeoldeforgevalley.com

THE WALK

After the car park, cross the road to a faint path then turn right on the road to **Hackness** (across the road at **Hazel Head** is a good viewpoint and an information board on the local geology). Continue along the road for half a mile, then immediately before the bridge, turn right (signposted "**Tabular Hills Walk**") along the **Sea Cut** (aka **North Back Drain**) used for flood control to take water from the River Derwent straight to the sea: that which misses the cut has to travel another 40 miles. **Raincliffe**

Guide to North Yorkshire Pub Walks

HOW TO GET THERE AND PARKING: East Ayton and West Ayton are 4 miles from Scarborough on the A170 to Pickering. From East Ayton take the road signposted to "Forge Valley, Hackness". Two miles along is a road junction and the small car park is by the right turn. The pub is on the A170 in West Ayton. **Sat Nav:** YO12 5TB.

MAP: OS Explorer Outdoor Leisure 27 North York Moors Eastern area. **Grid Ref:** SE 984875.

Woods are on the hillside to the right. After half a mile, drop down the bank to a stile and footbridge (easy to miss: it's by fencing enclosing a stream). Slant across (or go round) the field, then follow a track to the right of a plantation. Turn left at the junction of tracks and then take the right-hand track (ditch on left). Go right at the end of the second field (waymark), soon to reach a road.

2 Turn right for approximately 100m, then turn left ("**Public Bridleway**" sign but easily missed) into **Raincliffe Woods**. Follow the path up the wooded hillside for a quarter of a mile then, turn left along a broad well-used track. After less than a quarter of a mile go right where the track forks (wooden sculpture). The track crosses an open section (more sculptures), then returns to woodland. Approximately half a mile after the last turn, bear right (signposted bridleway) when the track divides again. Some quarter of a mile later (no sign, but look for an overgrown decrepit bench on the right), turn right on a path that climbs quite steeply through the woodland to reach the top in about a quarter of a mile.

3 Turn sharp right and walk along an attractive level path that runs just inside the woods with a field on the left (**Seamer Moor** where there are many tumuli). Initially, through the trees on the right, there are tantalising glimpses of the sea and **Scarborough**. Follow this path for 1¼ miles of pleasant easy walking. In moments of doubt, keep close to the field on the left and do not descend.

4 Leave the wood at a footpath gate (waymark) and follow a field path with an old stone wall on the left. Just before the gate, a tree-covered earthwork called **Skell Dikes** extends across the fields. The path descends gently and there are good views of the Yorkshire Wolds ahead. Keep

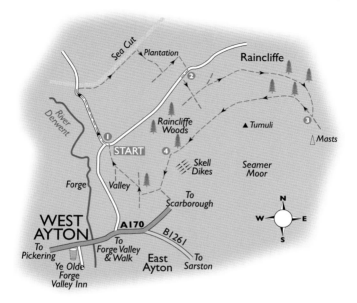

straight on at the junction of paths. Turn right when the path re-enters woodland (the wooded hillside of **Forge Valley**), and shortly afterwards turn left when the path forks. At the conveniently placed seat there is a splendid view across the valley. The path slants down the hillside and leads straight into the car park.

PLACES OF INTEREST NEARBY

There are parts of an Anglo-Saxon cross at **Hackness church** and some of the building dates back to the 11th century. One can trace much of England's seaside history in nearby **Scarborough** which developed on a magnificent site along the bays on either side of the Norman castle.

Robin Hood's Bay

16 Robin Hood's Bay

5 miles or 8 miles/8km or 12.8km

WALK HIGHLIGHTS
Picturesque Robin Hood's Bay, visits to the former Peak Alum Works (now a place of beauty and interest) and to Boggle Hole, and lots of glorious sea views.

THE PUB
The Victoria Hotel, Robin Hood's Bay, **YO22 4RL**
☎ 01947 880205 www.victoriarhb.com

THE WALK
The longer walk starts from Robin Hood's Bay and **the shorter walk** from point 3 near Boggle Hole.

1 From the car parks/bus stop, walk down to the old village and the sea, then turn right immediately before the **Old Coastguard Station Visitor Centre.** The path (**Cleveland Way**) drops down to a small seaside promenade, then climbs steps up the cliff. Go left at the junction of paths and climb more steps. Continue along the Cleveland Way as it follows the clifftop then drops steeply to **Boggle Hole**, close to the shore. Turn right and along the road for a few metres, then left along the **Cleveland Way** as it climbs more steps, levels out, then steps again as it descends to the **Stoupe Beck**.

HOW TO GET THERE AND PARKING: There are well signposted turns to Robin Hood's Bay from the A171 Scarborough/Whitby road. For Boggle Hole (narrow lane!) leave the A171 approximately 12 miles from Scarborough, seven from Whitby. Frequent Scarborough/Whitby bus service to/from Robin Hood's Bay. Robin Hood's Bay: two car parks (pay) in upper part of the village. **Sat Nav:** YO22 4RD. Boggle Hole: car park (donation) at end of the lane leading from A171. **Sat Nav:** YO22 4UQ.

MAP: OS Explorer Outdoor Leisure 27 North York Moors Eastern area. **Grid Ref:** NZ 950054 or NZ 953037.

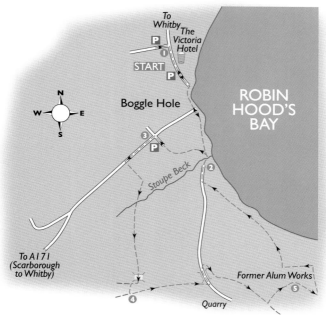

2 Turn right just before the footbridge and climb more steep steps. The path continues through a narrow meadow which leads into a green lane soon to reach crossroads by **Boggle Hole car park** where you turn left.

3 From the car park, walk along the tarmac lane away from the sea. After 300m, go over a ladder stile on the left (easily missed). Keep by the hedge on the right, and when the hedge ends go through bushes to a step stile (very easily missed). Slant right and down to the valley bottom. Cross the bridge over the **Stoupe Beck** then climb up the field past a gate on the left to a gate at the top left corner. Go straight up the next field to a stile by a gate, then in the following field keep by the hedge. Go under the bridge of the former Scarborough to Whitby railway line, turn right briefly, then left up a steep lane.

4 At the top, go left along another lane, climbing gently (sea views). After a third of a mile, turn sharp left (by a noticeboard) down a steeply-descending narrow tarmac lane, then immediately after the former railway bridge, turn right, then left along the track of the old line as it climbs towards **Ravenscar**. The banks are full of wild flowers in summer, and the sea views a delight. After half a mile turn left over a stile (easily missed) marked "**Conservation Walks**", and descend steeply. When the gradient levels, slant right to a gate. Turn right along an enclosed track, soon to reach a junction of paths.

5 Turn left down the path (**Cleveland Way**) to the **Alum Works**. Formerly a large, smoky and extremely smelly industrial enterprise and busy port, the National Trust site is now a place of beauty. The excellent information boards also mention adders! Leave by the path to the right of the red-pantiled building and follow the Cleveland Way across a field, then along the clifftop. After a mile, turn right on a tarmac road. Go past a small car park and along the Cleveland Way down to point 2. For the shorter walk turn left and follow the route from point 2 to the car park at point 3. For the longer route retrace your steps along the Cleveland Way back to **Robin Hood's Bay**.

PLACES OF INTEREST NEARBY

Wander the narrow streets of **Robin Hood's Bay**, and, if the time is right, watch the tide come in. Nearby **Whitby** is famous for its picturesque harbour and its clifftop abbey.

Grosmont Station

17 Grosmont & Goathland
4.5 miles or 7.5 miles/7.2km or 12km

WALK HIGHLIGHTS
An enjoyable walk through woods, meadows and moorland in the valley of the Musk Esk, with steam trains to goggle at or hear puffing and hissing behind the trees. You can do the whole 7.5 miles circuit, or walk from Grosmont to Goathland and return by train or vice versa.

THE PUB
The Station Tavern, Grosmont, **YO22 5PA**
☎ 01947 895060 www.stationtaverngrosmont.com

THE WALK
From the crossing gates, walk past the **Station Tavern** and up the steep village street. After about 300m, turn right down a footpath signposted "**Doctors Wood**". The woodland path crosses a footbridge to reach a tarmac lane where you turn left. Shortly after a gate, bear right (footpath sign) along a paved path which continues through the delightful **Crag Cliff Wood**. The path leaves the wood, crosses two fields, before briefly re-entering the wood, bending left, and running along the top of a meadow. The path enters further woodland, climbing a bank to

Guide to North Yorkshire Pub Walks

HOW TO GET THERE AND PARKING: 15 miles from Pickering on the A169 to Whitby turn left on minor road to Grosmont (steep descent). Park at the National Park car park at Grosmont (£4.50) a quarter of a mile from crossing gates on the road to Egton. **Sat Nav:** YO22 5QE.

MAP: OS Explorer Outdoor Leisure 27 North York Moors Eastern area. **Grid Ref:** NZ 827052.

a junction of paths where you turn left on a bridleway signposted **Goathland**. The bridleway goes to the hamlet of **Green End** where you turn left (waymarks).

2 Keep to the left of the houses, then turn right (bridleway sign) through the farmyard and along the farm track with a hedge on the right. The path keeps in the same direction across meadows to reach a tarmac road where you turn right. After a few metres (footpath sign) turn left along a level moorland path soon joined by a wall on the right. Turn right at a junction of paths and walk down to **Hill Farm**.

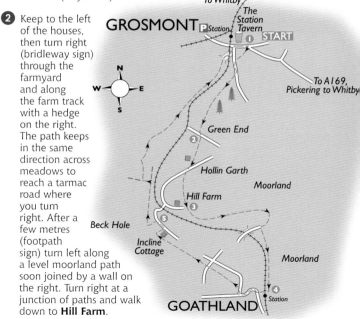

Turn left at Hill Farm along a level track past **Lins Farm**. Just before a seat on the right (recommended for view of the valley and railway), bear left on a path (de facto path on access land) that steadily climbs the moor. Go to the left of a house, straight on (waymark) where the access road bends left. Soon after, turn right and descend steeply in delightful surroundings. Turn right after the footbridge, then immediately before the ford, turn left on a grassy path that soon climbs steeply up the left side of the railway cutting before dropping down to **Goathland Station** (refreshments available).

Cross the line and walk up to **Goathland**. Turn right on the road to **Darnholme & Beck Hole**, then immediately after the car park, turn left along the "**Grosmont Rail Trail**". You are now on the old tramway, built by George Stephenson for horse-drawn traffic and opened in 1836. It closed in 1865 when the new line (or "deviation") replaced it. Keep along the former tramway for almost a mile, then shortly after Incline Cottage (a nice bit of early railway architecture), turn right (signpost) along the bridleway. When the road is reached, turn left into picturesque **Beck Hole** and past the pub.

Immediately after the bridge over the river, turn left on a footpath signed "**Musk Esk & Rail Trail**". Turn right when the tramway is rejoined and follow it to a waymarked post (a third of a mile) where you turn left through a gate marked "**Egton**" (or you can continue along the tramway). Cross the footbridge on the right and follow through meadows a pleasant but little-used waymarked path which keeps close to the fence and river on the right before rejoining the tramway. Continue along the tramway till it ends, then follow the path up the hillside with views below of trains and engine sheds. Turn right at the top (good view of **Grosmont**), left on the **Rail Trail** past the church soon to come into Grosmont at the crossing gates.

PLACES OF INTEREST NEARBY

The **North York Moors Railway** runs frequent trains on its scenic 18-mile route between Grosmont and Pickering. Most of the trains are steam-hauled, sometimes by famous engines. Some trains now go on to Whitby.

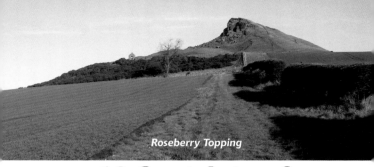

Roseberry Topping

18 Great Ayton & Roseberry Topping

4 miles or 7 miles/6.4km or 11.2km

WALK HIGHLIGHTS

An interesting, well-wooded walk with an ascent of the shapely peak of Roseberry Topping (320 metres), one of the best viewpoints in Yorkshire. The walk can be extended to include Captain Cook's Monument.

THE PUB

The Royal Oak, Great Ayton, **TS9 6BW**
☎ 01642 722361 www.royaloakgreatayton.co.uk

THE WALK

1 Walk up to the top of **Great Ayton**'s attractive main street, keep straight on (**Newton Road**) at the road junction, and soon go through the kissing gate on the right. Follow the enclosed path through meadows and bands of woodland (good views of the surrounding countryside) and over the level crossing to **Cliff Ridge Wood** (National Trust) which cloaks a former quarry from which whinstone (a volcanic rock) was extracted.

2 At the junction of paths by the information board go straight across to the narrow path that slants up the wooded hillside. At the top of the wood, the path briefly turns left, then with **Roseberry Topping** now in view, follows a fence on the right. Slant left of the trees when a field is

56

HOW TO GET THERE AND PARKING: Great Ayton is on the A173 Stokesley to Guisborough road, and seven miles south-east of Middlesbrough. The Royal Oak is on the main street (High Street). There is roadside parking or a small car park at the top of the main street. **Sat Nav:** TS9 6PN.

MAP: OS Explorer Outdoor Leisure 26 North York Moors: Western area. **Grid Ref:** NZ 563107.

reached, then follow the clear path on a bee-line for Roseberry Topping rearing up ahead like a miniature Matterhorn. The unusual small building on the left is a restored 18th-century shooting box. Keep by the fence on the right, then turn left up the steep paved path to the top. There's a terrific view: the Cleveland Hills, across the Tees plain to the Pennines, Middlesbrough – and the sea!

For the shorter walk (4 miles), retrace steps off the summit, and go down the gully just to the right of the shooting box. After the gate into **Newton Wood** turn left along the top of the wood. Fork right when the path divides (a quarter of a mile). The path slants down the hillside, bears left at the bottom, then keeps close to the edge of the wood

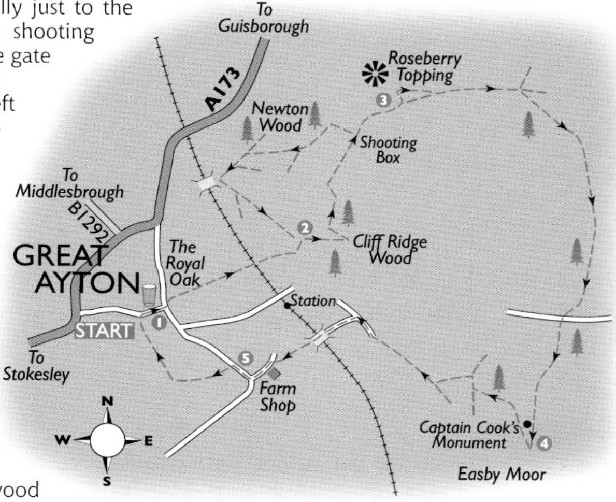

To Guisborough

A173

Roseberry Topping

Newton Wood

Shooting Box

To Middlesbrough

B1292

The Royal Oak

GREAT AYTON

Station

START

To Stokesley

Cliff Ridge Wood

Farm Shop

Captain Cook's Monument

Easby Moor

N
W — E
S

to reach a T-junction with a broad track where you turn left. After a few metres you pass the entrance to the former whinstone quarry (the information board gives a fascinating account of its geology and history). Take the path to the left of the National Trust sign, and, after ½ mile of attractive woodland walking, point 2 is reached again (easily missed!). Turn right and with views of the Cleveland Hills retrace steps to **Great Ayton**.

For the longer walk (7 miles), keep along the ridge after the summit, then descend the steep paved path. At the bottom, keep in the same direction by the fence/wall on the right soon to climb steeply on to **Newton Moor**. Bear right at the signpost at the top, and along an attractive level moorland path (**Cleveland Way**) still by the fence/wall on the right. Drop down to the road at **Gribdale**, and go straight across right to a broad track which climbs through conifers then moorland to Captain Cook's Monument erected in 1827 in memory of "the celebrated circumnavigator".

④ Turn sharp right on a narrow path that goes between two stone gateposts. Shortly after, at a junction of paths, bear left on a woodland path that soon descends steeply. Beyond the wood the path soon turns right (waymark post) through the gorse and slants down the hillside. Shortly after a wooded section (beware mud and tree roots), turn left down a lane signed "**Weak Bridge**". Cross the offending railway construction and continue along the lane past **Fletcher's Farm Shop** to a road junction.

⑤ Turn right, then immediately after the first house on the left, turn left along an enclosed path (footpath sign). Go over the footbridge across the **River Leven**, keep by the fence on the right, then cross the field to the footpath gate at the far end. The path cuts across the uncultivated corner of the next field, then, by the hedge on the right, goes straight back to **Great Ayton**. Just before the bridge, aficionados of such artefacts may note the Victorian urinal (now locked! – modern version just across the road).

PLACES OF INTEREST NEARBY

The whole area is full of Captain Cook associations including a museum in **Great Ayton**. He was born in 1728 at nearby Marton and the family moved to Great Ayton in 1736.

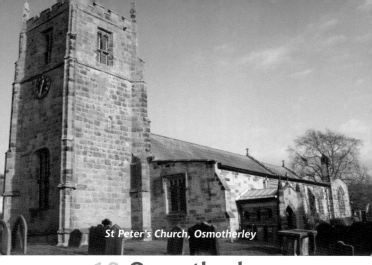

St Peter's Church, Osmotherley

19 Osmotherley

5 miles/8km

WALK HIGHLIGHTS

Moorland, meadow and woodland with lots of good views. Osmotherley is a village of interest and charm, a place to linger. Its well-concealed church, dating from the 12th century, is at the back of the pub.

THE PUB

The Queen Catherine Hotel, Osmotherley, **DL6 3AG**
☎ 01609 883209 www.queencatherinehotel.co.uk

THE WALK

1 From the T-junction in the middle of **Osmotherley** village go straight across beyond the bus shelter to a ginnel with a noticeboard above saying "Osmotherly Methodist Church 1754". The path (also the **Cleveland Way**) crosses a back lane, continues as an enclosed path across fields then drops down steeply to a footbridge over the **Cod Beck**.

Guide to North Yorkshire Pub Walks

HOW TO GET THERE AND PARKING: Signposted turn from the A19, nine miles north of Thirsk. Bus services from Northallerton and Middlesbrough. The Queen Catherine is on the right just before the main road junction in the middle of the village. Street parking. **Sat Nav:** DL6 3AG.

MAP: OS Explorer Outdoor Leisure 26 North York Moors Western area. **Grid Ref:** SE 455972.

2 A few metres after the footbridge, turn left on an access track (waymark). After a short distance, go through a footpath gate on the left and follow the path that slants up the hillside. It bears left just to the left of the house and outbuilding, soon goes through a gate, then a footpath gate. If in doubt, keep just above the pylons. At the far side of the next field, immediately before a gate (waymark post), turn right on to the track up the hillside by a house on the left. Go through a gate, keep straight on past farm buildings to go through another gate, then continue up the hillside by the hedge on the left.

3 Turn left at the top (look back for good views) on to a green lane called **Green Lane**, then soon (just before a house – "**Rocky Plain**") go through a footpath gate on the right which soon joins with the access road ascending the hillside. Turn left at the T-junction at the top, and follow the broad unmade road, soon with woodland on the left. Nothing special at first, it gradually becomes a splendid moorland track with good views ahead. After a mile it drops down to a footbridge and ford over **Cod Beck** (an attractive spot) to join a road.

4 Go left along the road. After less than a quarter of a mile, opposite the second car park, turn right by a tall stone post (carved "**Lyke Wake Walk**", a 42-mile route to Ravenscar). Follow the clear path up **Scarth Wood Moor** to the top left corner from where (convenient seat) the **Cleveland Hills** and **Roseberry Topping** come into view. The path is an ad hoc path on access land.

5 Turn left along the **Cleveland Way** (it's also the **Coast to Coast Path**), go through two gates and follow the path across **Beacon Hill** (299m), trig point over the wall on the left. Good views south and east, the rest blocked out by trees. The path, just inside woodland, is a delight. It gradually descends **Beacon Hill** and there's a good viewpoint westwards at a gap in the trees. Ignore the Coast to Coast as it departs to the right. At the farm, veer slightly left along the access road. At the T-junction, turn right and walk into **Osmotherley**. On the right, you will pass the village pinfold where stray cattle were impounded and returned to owner by payment of a fine to the pinder.

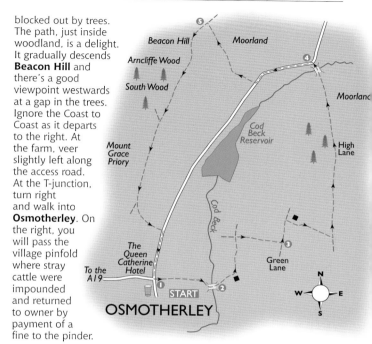

PLACES OF INTEREST NEARBY

Less than three miles away, in a secluded setting just beneath Beacon Hill is **Mount Grace Priory**. Founded in 1398, English Heritage describes it as "much the best-preserved Carthusian priory in England". Seven miles away is **Northallerton**, North Yorkshire's county town, a place of modest size with a fine and typically North Yorkshire high street.

The White Horse at Kilburn

20 Kilburn White Horse

6 miles/9.6km

WALK HIGHLIGHTS

A walk of stunning views and attractive woodland paths. Sutton Bank is one of the best viewpoints in the land. Kilburn White Horse can be seen from miles away (including the outskirts of Leeds).

THE PUB

The Forresters Arms Hotel, Kilburn, **YO61 4AH**
☎ 01347 868386 www.forrestersarms.com

THE WALK

1 Turn right after leaving the car park and walk down the road. Turn left when a track crosses the road after about 300m, then immediately turn right on a woodland path close to the road. After returning to the road, and just after a small car park on your right, turn right through the footpath gate beside farm gate.

2 Follow the bridleway for approximately a mile, ignoring side paths. Go

HOW TO GET THERE AND PARKING: From Thirsk follow A170 Scarborough road and half a mile after the top of Sutton Bank turn right on minor road signposted "Yorkshire Gliding Club White Horse". After a mile the road descends steeply, and the car park is on the right just below the White Horse. The road continues to Kilburn and the Forresters Arms is in the middle of the village. **Sat Nav:** YO61 4AN.

MAP: OS Explorer Outdoor Leisure 26 North York Moors Western area. **Grid Ref:** SE 514812.

straight ahead when it is joined by a wide track. Bear left at the junction of tracks immediately after a brief descent. Watch out for a field on the right, and shortly afterwards a signpost on the right (easily missed) saying "**Bridleway Hood Grange/ A170**". The bridleway goes down a field towards the right-hand side of the farm ahead (**Hood Grange**) with good views of **Sutton Bank**. Turn left at the bottom of the field (sign), then over the footbridge. Climb the

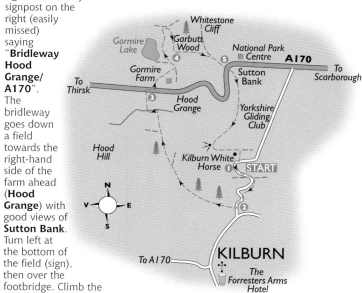

Guide to North Yorkshire Pub Walks

hillside, cross the farm road and follow the path up to the A170.

3 Turn right along the A170 (wide verge) for 100m, then go over a stile on the left by a gate saying "**No Sledging**". The path slants across the field as it climbs the low hill ahead. Cross into the next field via a step stile (post and waymark), then slant left (do not descend!) to a farm gate which leads into an enclosed track. At **Gormire Farm** turn right between the buildings, then immediately (well signed) turn left on to a green lane that soon leads to a junction of paths (signpost).

4 Turn right to "**Southwoods**". Follow the path beside tree-lined **Gormire Lake** (formed by glacial deposits) and continue on the woodland path for a further third of a mile. A few metres before a junction of bridleways (signpost) turn sharp right (no sign) up a clear path climbing the wooded hillside. Soon go over a stile into **Garbutt Wood** signposted "**Sloping Path**". The path keeps more or less level along the hillside in the delightful woodland of the **Yorkshire Wildlife Trust nature reserve**. At a junction of paths after about a third of a mile, turn left on a path that climbs the cliff on a sloping route. There are a few steep sections, some fairly level stretches and several delightful views – a most enjoyable climb. At the top, turn right along the Cleveland Way soon to reach the A170 close to the **National Park Centre** (well worth visiting) at the top of **Sutton Bank**.

5 Cross the A170 and bear right on the scenic route when the path divides (soon reunites). The final mile is exhilarating walking on a popular path with wide views across the **Vale of York**. The best view of all is from the very end of the edge where you enjoy a prospect stretching from the Wolds in the south east to the Pennines in the west. A grandstand finish! Follow the path at the top of the **White Horse**, and when it divides bear right to a flight of steps and the car park.

PLACES OF INTEREST NEARBY

Coxwold, two miles from Kilburn, is noted for its association with Laurence Sterne, author of *Tristram Shandy*. Sterne was the vicar of Coxwold from 1760 until his death in 1768 and lived at Shandy Hall, now a small museum.